GROWING AND STORING HERBS

A herb garden is within everyone's reach, for these useful and handsome plants can be grown in everything from a window box to a large formal garden. This book describes how to grow herbs successfully and how to dry and store them for use through the winter.

Also by Brian Walkden
FOOD FROM YOUR GARDEN

GROWING AND STORING HERBS

How to Ensure Your Own Year-Round Supply of
Culinary Flavourings

by
Brian and Mary Walkden

Herb illustrations from
A Complete Culinary Herbal
(illustrated and written by
Audrey Wynne Hatfield)

THORSONS PUBLISHERS LIMITED
Wellingborough, Northamptonshire

First published 1979
Second Impression 1980

ISBN 0 7225 0509 4 (hardback)
ISBN 0 7225 0508 6 (paperback)

Photoset by Specialised Offset Services Limited, Liverpool
and printed in Great Britain by
Weatherby Woolnough, Wellingborough, Northamptonshire
on paper made from 100% re-cycled fibre supplied by
P.F Bingham Ltd., Croydon, Surrey

CONTENTS

1

THE VERSATILITY OF HERBS

Herbs have been used for culinary, cosmetic and medicinal purposes for centuries; in fact, their uses have not changed a lot since the 15th-century lady's maid brewed a tisane for 'my lady's headache'. The aroma and flavour of cooking with herbs will bring an appreciative response from the family, and you can pick up new ideas on holidays spent abroad, for using herbs in foreign recipes to add to your repertoire.

Most herbs are easy to grow and maintain, even with a fair share of neglect, and all can add subtle perfume and colour to the existing garden as well as being useful into the bargain. Added attractions are the butterflies and bees, who love to feed on the aromatic flowers and leaves of the plants. So there is the bonus of helping to conserve our insect life as well.

There is no need for a special part of the garden to be set aside purely for herb cultivation, though if you have a small area near the kitchen, this would be an ideal spot for a herb garden. Many herbs are very attractive and grow so compactly that they can be used in the formal garden as edgings to borders and paths, and to outline beds of flowers. Some, like the Bay tree, can become focal points of interest in the garden, or can make a splendid entrance to the front door, especially if planted in tubs. The Bay is a slow-growing evergreen tree, which only needs clipping occasionally to keep it in good shape.

Herbs for edgings could be Chives, Marjoram and Thyme, which need very little space. These are all perennial and so will be with you for life. Rosemary, an evergreen which likes the sun, can be trained against a warm wall or grown in a tub.

Herbs to be incorporated in the herbaceous border include Fennel, which reaches a height of 8 feet (2.6m), with most attractive bright green or bronze feathery foliage; Angelica, also 8 feet (2.6m) tall, with clusters of yellow-green flowers; and Lovage, which is a slow grower and likes plenty of sun. Borage is one that can be planted in the centre of the border and has intense blue flowers. The leaves of Borage, when used young, are cucumber-flavoured and are delicious in salads.

Why not grow Thyme on your paths? It is a most accommodating plant, which can be planted in the crevices between paving stones, and releases a very pungent odour when trodden under foot.

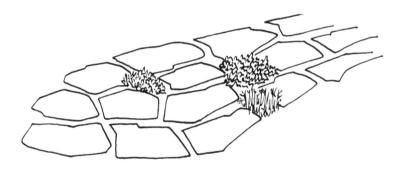

Herbs such as Thyme grown in small clumps in a crazy paving path — aromatic when trodden on.

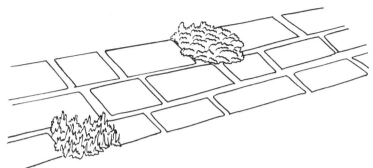

With paving slabs odd pieces can be left out and a clump of low-growing herbs can be planted in the space.

Most of these herbs can be bought in packets, dried, in any supermarket, but what is more satisfying than being able to pick your own fresh herbs whenever you like, and also to dry or freeze them when the time is right? Herbs used in cooking stimulate the appetite, and the cheaper cuts of meat can be made more interesting and edible by their addition. The runner bean is transformed by the use of Tarragon, salads enlivened by the inclusion of Marjoram and Basil, and a Bay leaf added to the old stand-by, rice pudding, lifts it into the cordon bleu class. By getting to know your herbs, you can mix various types together and use them, according to your taste, in soups and stews.

Medicinal Uses

Medicinally, herbs really come into their own. They are gentle in use, can do no harm and have no cumulative effect. Recently there has been a marked change from the mass-produced pills and potions to natural herbs and substances. An infusion of Dill seeds, for instance, makes the old fashioned Dill water which is good for the digestion, whilst an infusion of Balm leaves acts as a tonic as well as helping the digestion. Basil is also used for digestive upsets, and for baths and soothing compresses.

Insomniacs are often helped to sleep by using a herb pillow; the natural perfumes and oils that are released with the heat of the body aid relaxation. Another remedy for sleeplessness is herb tea taken before retiring. An infusion of leaves of Balm, Bergamot, Chamomile, and Lemon Verbena in boiling water provides a fragrant, relaxing drink. An old Countryman's recipe for bee and wasp stings was to apply the bruised leaves of Summer Savory to the affected area for instant relief.

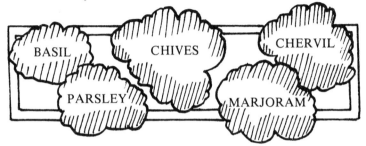

Herb plants for a window box.

Most of these herbs that we have mentioned can be grown in small areas, such as window boxes, pots and tubs. Ideally, there is nothing like having a well-designed herb garden, but in these days of high-rise flats you can still have a useful herb plot on the window-sill. Basil, Chervil, Chives, Marjoram and Parsley will grow quite happily in window boxes and pots on a sunny window-sill in the kitchen. A good idea is to take fresh cuttings each autumn. Mint is best left in a container of its own, as it soon takes over and strangles any other plant planted with it. Parsley is quite at home indoors as long as it is well watered. Bay, as we have said before, can be grown in a tub, either outside the front door or on a patio. As exposure to north and east winds can cause the leaves to brown at the edges, it is a good plan to plant it in a sheltered, sunny position. Also for use on the patio is the terracotta parsley pot, designed exclusively for the cultivation of parsley. This can be most attractive when smothered in the crinkly green heads of parsley, especially if mixed among other pot-grown plants and herbs.

Even the smallest garden can afford a corner to be given over to growing herbs. These, of course, would have to be the most common ones used in cooking and ones that have a compact, bushy habit. As long as the site is in a sunny position, they are quite indifferent about the soil.

Herb Lore Through the Ages
Herb lore has been passed down from medieval times, from the lady of the manor in her stillroom, with her possets and simples, to the present day space-age lady with her micro-wave oven. Medicinally, they go back 2,700 years; they are described in Chinese herbals and the Ancient Egyptians were known to use herbs for their medicinal properties. In Britain, most exotic and aromatic plants were unknown in Anglo-Saxon times, but the herbs that grew wild in the countryside were put to medicinal as well as culinary use.

Some of their names reflect the use to which they were put, such as lung wort, liver wort, cough wort, and woundwort; 'wort' meant 'plant'. Most monasteries had a herb or 'infirmary' garden and by carefully blending and distilling various mixtures of herbs, they discovered fragrant and delicious liqueurs, such as Benedictine and Chartreuse. Even today, some of these recipes remain a secret known only to the monks of the abbeys that distill the liqueurs. In eighth-century France, Charlemagne ordered all the imperial farms to grow herbs.

Herbs and spices have been used in cooking for hundreds of years. In medieval times, of course, they disguised the flavour of meat that had seen better days, but the flavours became popular in their own right, and the housewife of today wants to have fresh, frozen or dried herbs at her elbow to give her cooking that extra 'zing'.

2

PLANNING A HERB GARDEN

Years ago, the herb garden was a feature of its own, like the herbaceous border and the sunken rose garden. Nowadays, it has to fit in with its surroundings and so has become smaller, but has lost none of its charm.

A lot will depend on the style of garden you have, too. If it is a formal one, you want a formal herb garden, but if you have an informal layout then you can plan for a natural type of area where the beds or borders have sweeps or curves – in fact, something reminiscent of the old-fashioned cottage garden. Even if you can only make a narrow border, you will be able to get at least one row of plants in, but if you have the space do try and make a wide border, which is far more interesting. Herb garden planning is very similar to planning an herbaceous border where you have at least three or four rows of plants. You can of course be really ambitious and try and imitate the herb gardens of old which were complete gardens in themselves with paths leading into and around them and generous borders of plants. If you do have such a garden, you should try and keep the pathway as natural as possible – old bricks or old paving stones or the modern type with rough faced surfaces are ideal for paths.

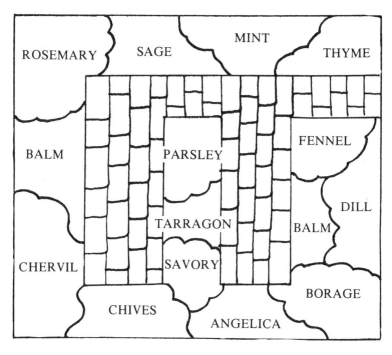

Formal herb garden layout using paving slabs for the pathways and easy access to all beds. Herbs planted in bold sweeps.

Ideally, herbs should be grown in close proximity to the kitchen, so that it takes no time to pop out and pick whatever is needed. However, this is often impracticable, unless the kitchen faces south and is sheltered from wind and frost. Herbs like a sunny, sheltered position, and a bed measuring 6 feet x 6 feet (1.8m x 1.8m) can accommodate the most popular varieties. Plants can be grown in irregularly-shaped areas, dovetailing into each other and forming a pleasing effect of leaf shape and colour.

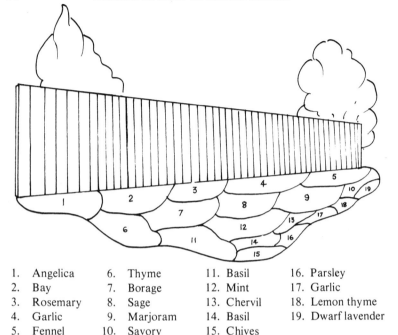

1. Angelica	6. Thyme	11. Basil	16. Parsley
2. Bay	7. Borage	12. Mint	17. Garlic
3. Rosemary	8. Sage	13. Chervil	18. Lemon thyme
4. Garlic	9. Marjoram	14. Basil	19. Dwarf lavender
5. Fennel	10. Savory	15. Chives	

Fence/hedge background with herb bed laid out in a series of pleasing sweeps and curves. Low-growing plants towards the front; taller ones towards the back of the border.

If you are artistic you can go to town on creating herb borders of different outlines. You could, in fact, have a type of cartwheel effect with the borders radiating out from a central specimen plant. Quite intricate designs can be created, based on the Elizabethan Knot gardens, and you can produce beautiful patterns of borders and plants if you put pen to paper and draw them out accurately beforehand.

The amount of room you should allocate for your herb garden will depend on the types of plants you want to grow and the descriptions of plants in Chapters 4 and 5 will guide you in this respect. A plant growing only a few inches high can be packed close together with similar plants, but the taller ones that grow anything up to 2 or 3 feet (60cm-1m) high need much more space around them. One interesting system which overcomes the problem of heights and spreads is to grow plants in little plots about 1 yard (1m) square.

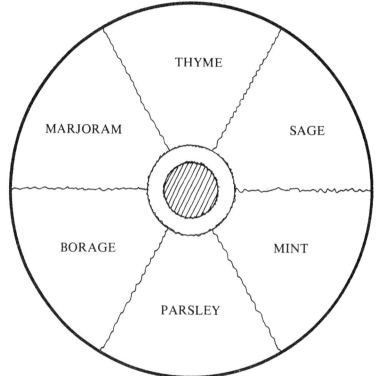

Another eye-catching design. A circle of herbs with a centre-piece of a statue or sundial. Ideal for a lawn setting.

Paths and Surrounds

Paving stones laid in the form of a cross, with plants growing in between the arms, enable the herbs to be picked more easily. Another arrangement is to grow plants in blocks, rather like a chess-board. Squares filled with plants alternate with squares filled with gravel or even with paving stones. Plants that vary in height can be grown near to each other and will not encroach or overshadow their smaller neighbours. It is a good idea to plan a herb bed with a brick or paving surround, so that in inclement

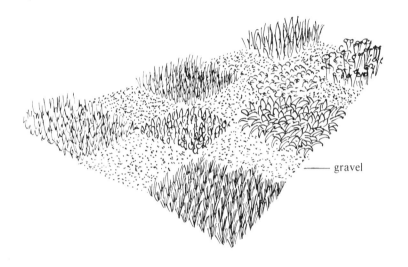

gravel

Layout for a herb garden in chess-board formation.

weather, your feet are kept dry and there is no need to trample on the bed when picking. The next design has diamond-shaped beds, and the shapes are outlined in box. This has the advantage of keeping each herb separate from the others.

A sundial, bird bath, a statue, or even a small flowering tree set in the centre of a grass plot, surrounded by four borders of mixed herbs, would make an eye-catching feature of the herb garden. The amount of shade cast by the tree would have to be carefully considered before planting. Here, the borders could be

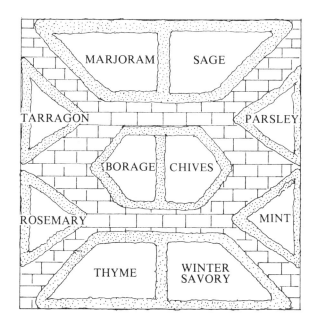

Attractive layout for a more ambitious herb garden.

planted with a vast range of plants, from the giant Foxgloves, Fennel and Angelica down to the smaller Thyme, Chives and Marjoram. If Sage is grown close to the edge of the border, the bruising of the leaves by the lawnmower throws out a rich perfume.

Finding Room in a Small Garden

If it is impossible to find room for a special herb garden, many herbs can be grown in the herbaceous border. It is advisable however, to ascertain the eventual height of your chosen herbs, so that the taller ones are situated at the back of the border and the smaller ones in front.

Herbs used for a neat edging to the border are very attractive.

The golden Marjoram, for instance, will associate beautifully with white, blue and mauve neighbours; violets or pansies will thread their way through the shiny yellow leaves of Marjoram. Thyme and Marjoram have the advantage of being evergreen and so will go on all through the year.

If space is reduced to a minimum, a specimen tree, like the Bay, which is evergreen, can become a focal point in the garden. Even Rosemary used as a shrub, either in a tub or trained against a warm wall, is most attractive as it is evergreen and has lots of bright blue flowers. On the patio, too, herbs can be grown in pots, troughs and tubs. Lemon Verbena, Myrtle, Parsley, Mint (lemon and apple), Chives, Chervil, and of course Rosemary and Bay, are all subjects for pot and trough culture. These will grow quite happily with any other plants you may have on the patio. The scented leaf Geraniums too are ideal for patio growing, but these are tender plants and need protection against frost in winter.

Herbs

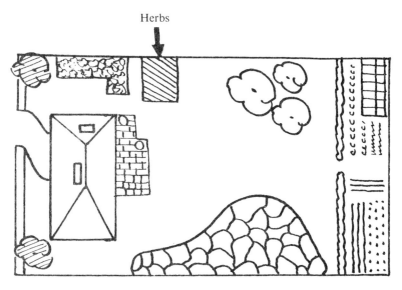

Herb plot (6ft x 6ft) close by kitchen for convenience.

The vegetable garden is another obvious place for kitchen herbs. These can be grown in rows between crops, but herbs like Mint which have underground stems need to be confined in a box or container, otherwise they soon pop up all over the place and can become a nuisance.

Flat-dwellers need not sigh with envy over garden-owners; they too can have quite a selection of herbs growing happily on a sunny window-sill in window boxes, troughs or pots. The range is obviously limited, but most of the popular and well-used ones can be grown. Chervil, Basil, Mint, Chives, Parsley, and pot Marjoram are just a few of the easily grown ones. They will not last indefinitely kept indoors, so it is advisable to take fresh cuttings each autumn. The golden rule is to keep picking, as this encourages the new young leaves to grow.

If a larger, more ambitious scheme for a herb garden is to be contemplated, it is a good idea to draw a detailed plan of the site before putting a spade into the ground. If the plot is large, a paved herb garden is attractive, as the colour of the stones will blend and contrast with the herbs themselves, thus providing a perfect background for them. The beds within the paved area can be of any shape, and many fascinating and unusual herbs can be incorporated. Standard Honeysuckles, Lemon Verbena in a tub, even a seat surrounded by a Southern Wood hedge and shaded by a Bay tree are features that could be put into the design. Visits to gardens open to the public which have historical herb gardens often help you to envisage a design which can be carried out in a smaller style.

Grouping the Plants

Once you have decided on the plants you wish to grow, you should group them according to their eventual heights and then sketch out their positions in little groups or plots. You can make good use of plants' heights or spreads for their actual positionings in your herb garden. For example, a herb garden or

border situated against a wall or fence could have the taller
plants towards the back, concealing the background, with the
smaller plants towards the front of the border, along similar lines
to the flower border schemes. You can also dot some of the
taller plants here and there to give height, character and interest
to a border.

There is a lot to be said, too, for using plants according to
their spread and also according to their leaf formation. The
bushier or trailing plants could be situated towards the front of
the border, allowing some of the growth to trail attractively and
naturally along the pathways. The ferny types, with a more
delicate type of foliage, could be situated near plants which have
broad, bold foliage, so that the contrast is unusual and eye-
catching. For example, Parsley could be planted near to Mint,
and the two foliages will make an effective contrast.

Planting

Once you have made your plan on paper, it can be transferred
quite easily on to the actual site by marking out with cane stick
labels and scratching out the areas of each clump of plants with
the end of a cane stick. It is then a simple matter to plant or sow
in the respective positions, checking back from your plan.

If your garden is exposed to strong winds, this will have to be
planned for. Here some form of wind break or shelter is
advisable and this can be used as part of your planting or layout
scheme. For example, an attractive wooden fence could be
erected against which some of your taller herb plants could be
trained. You could even use screen walling units, which by the
very tracery of their pattern or design add to the effect of a
natural herb garden. Or you could plant one or two shrubs or
even a hedge to block out the cold winds and protect the herb
garden. A large herb garden can be a place in which to sit and
relax, so some form of shelter for the plants could also be a
shelter for you to keep the cold winds off you when reclining in
that comfortable chair. Do not forget, though, that you must

pay close attention to light when erecting a fence or shelter; under no circumstances should such a shelter block valuable light to your herb garden plants, otherwise they will become weak and badly drawn.

3

BASIC PREPARATIONS

Herbs, on the whole, are not fussy about soil and will usually flourish in any garden. They thrive on well-drained light soil, and some, like Marjoram and Thyme, prefer chalky ground, while others, such as Angelica, Bergamot, Chamomile, and Mint, prefer the heavier soils. But all like a sunny position. They should be planted in a spot that faces south and is sheltered to the north and east from wind and frost.

If the site is established, see that the ground is weed-free and rake down to a fine tilth before marking out and planting. All that is necessary then is a light dressing of lime in the autumn and a general purpose fertilizer in the spring. If the ground is new or neglected, dig it over well, clearing all grass and weeds, especially the perennial ones like couch grass and ground elder. Rake level and to a fine tilth, and give the soil a light dressing of fertilizer. If the soil is heavy or sticky, fork in about two bucketfuls of mortar rubble or wood ash to the square yard, and this will make it a lot lighter.

Badly Drained Ground
One thing that most herbs do not like is badly drained ground.

There can be a little difficulty, too, if your soil happens to be rather heavy or is a sticky type of clay. In these circumstances you will have to pay very strict attention to the initial soil preparations.

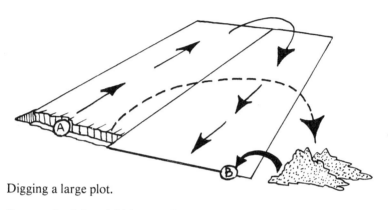

Digging a large plot.

Excavated soil from initial trench (A) placed at end of plot where digging will finish (B). Digging follows route of arrows – up one half of plot and down the other.

This type of ground should be dug as deeply as possible so that the plants will have a good open root run, and the soil is as broken up and as well drained as possible. The only problem with deep digging is that there is a danger of bringing to the surface poor sub-soil stratas. You must therefore make an experimental dig initially to discover what sort of soil you have below, say, 8 inches (20cm). If this soil is reasonable, then it is a good plan to take out a trench about 10 inches (25cm) deep or to the full depth of the digging spade, and about 1 foot (30cm) wide.

The soil excavated from the trench should be taken in the wheelbarrow to the end of the plot where your cultivations will end. It should be tipped in a neat heap and will be used to fill up your last trench.

If the site is to be a wide one, it is helpful to divide the border into two halves, digging down one half and coming back on the other half. Dig by throwing the soil forward into the open trench and when you have dug another trench in this way, the base of the open trench should be broken up with a fork. It would be a good plan at this stage to work in some rotten manure or even some sharp sand or well weathered cinders – anything, in fact, to keep the soil open.

Winter Weathering

Leave the soil as rough as possible, and preferably do your digging in the late autumn or winter so that the completed area can be subjected to the rigours of the winter, when the action of frost and winds in particular will help to break the surface soil down.

It is quite amazing the difference it makes to dig in the winter and allow for this weathering. The soil will then rake down very easily in the spring when you get ready for sowing or planting.

If your soil is particularly heavy and sticky and you are only going to grow a few herbs, it might pay you to produce raised beds. This means marking out the required herb garden area or bed area, digging this over as deeply as possible and then importing some more soil, either from another part of the garden, or preferably some which you can buy from a local source, and tipping this on top. This will be your good growing soil. It will be several inches above the surrounding ground and should be a well-drained site.

Adding Organic Matter

You cannot beat having the maximum amount of organic matter in your herb bed soil. This can take the form of rotted manure (which must be very well rotted indeed), composted vegetable waste or moist peat. Even composted leaves from the autumn leaf fall will be most useful. This compost or organic matter is a natural plant food and it also helps to improve the condition or the structure of the soil. The more organic matter you can put into a stubborn soil, the easier it will be to work in time.

Organic matter is of vital importance for moisture conservation. In fact, it acts very like a sponge, holding every valuable drop of moisture for as long as possible. Your herb plants will appreciate this, especially during a hot dry summer. If you have a light sandy type of soil, the incorporation of organic matter is most important because these soils tend to dry out rapidly and they must have some substance in them to hold moisture for as long as possible. There is another plus factor too, which is that the compost or organic matter encourages a vigorous root formation; the more roots a herb plant has, the healthier it will be because it can forage better for food nutrients as well as for its moisture.

Growing in Containers

Soil preparation also has to be considered for herbs to be grown in containers. The first requisite is for good drainage and a container must have drainage holes. If it has not got them already, you will have to make some. Drainage holes must have some broken crocks or stones placed carefully over them to prevent soil blocking the holes and yet allow water to percolate through. A layer of $\frac{1}{2}$ inch (1cm) or so of small stones or crocks is ideal, followed by the growing medium or soil. If you are not using many containers, the simplest method is to buy some potting compost, conveniently packed in carry-home plastic bags, which you can get from your local shop or garden centre. Choose one which contains all the essential nutrients for good plant growth.

You can of course make up your own compost at home by using 3 parts good quality soil to 1-$1\frac{1}{2}$ parts horticultural peat which must be dampened before it is worked in, plus 1-$1\frac{1}{2}$ oz (25-35g) of a general or balanced fertilizer to every bushel of the soil and peat mix. A bushel is conveniently measured in a box with inside dimensions of 22 x 10 x 10 inches (65 x 25 x 25cm).

Make sure, when you are preparing your own compost, that you sieve the soil well so that large stones and so on are removed. A fine sieve should not be used, otherwise the soil will tend to become too compacted in the containers.

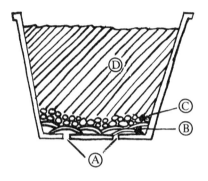

A   Drainage holes.
B   Broken crocks cover the
      drainage holes to prevent
      soil blockage.
C   Shallow layer of small stones.
D   Growing medium.

Preparing a container.

A word of warning about the peat. Although peat is an invaluable organic material, it is very difficult to moisten once it dries out badly, so do make sure that it is well damped down before you add it to the soil mix.

Growing in Cavity Walls
Because herbs are very attractive garden plants, it is a nice idea to grow some in cavity walls. These are double-sided walls, usually low, with a soil interior. A width of at least 12-19 inches (30-45cm) of soil is necessary, and it should be as deep as possible, the minimum depth being 12-15 inches (30-37cm). As with the containers, soil in a cavity wall can dry out quickly, so

use the mixtures recommended, and of course also keep an eye on watering during the growing period. The ideal aim is to keep your soil mixture just nicely moist at all times. Although most herbs will grow on ground which is not too rich, it is always advisable to provide some basic plant food in order to promote good, steady growth and the balanced or general fertilizer is ideal for this. Some of the liquid feeds are also excellent; they can be mixed in water and applied during the growing period.

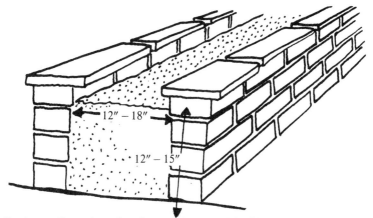

Cavity wall section showing minimum width/depth of soil for herb culture.

If you want to make up your own 'secret' formula for plant food, gather together the following ingredients: sulphate of ammonia, super phosphate of lime, sulphate of potash and steamed bone flour. The proportions required are as follows: sulphate of ammonia, 5 parts by weight; super phosphate of lime, 7 parts by weight; sulphate of potash, 2 parts by weight; and steamed bone flour, 1 part by weight. Steamed bone flour can be left out if you find it difficult to get hold of. All the ingredients should then be mixed well together and used prior to planting or sowing at the rate of $1\frac{1}{2}$-2 oz (35-50g) per square yard (square metre). This is a very well balanced fertilizer.

Design and Construction

If you are really going to town and making a large herb garden or a feature of herbs in your garden, it is important to familiarize yourself with certain materials which are necessary to complete the whole picture. One of the main ingredients of a herb garden layout is the paths. The materials for paths, if they are to be in keeping with the old-fashioned atmosphere you are trying to create, should be chosen carefully.

Brick, Gravel or Paved Paths

One very good material to use is old bricks, which can be cleaned up and used to make some delightful path designs. Because they are small, you can devise some very intriguing and delightful patterns with them; for example, very eye-catching patterns can be achieved by setting some of the bricks on their edges and others flat. With permutations of this arrangement

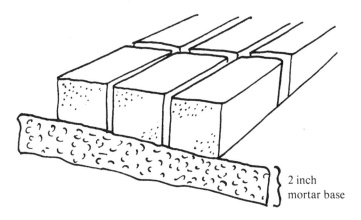

Path from old bricks set on a 2 inch mortar foundation.

and by placing the bricks at angles to each other, you can produce a very attractive path. The bricks can be set on well firmed ground, but for safety's sake and for minimum maintenance, especially with regard to weed control, the bricks should be set in a 2-inch (5cm) mortar or cement bedding.

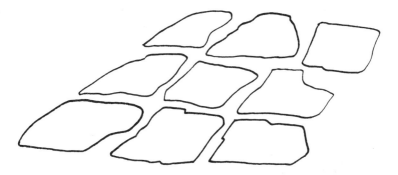

Crazy paving makes a nice natural type of pathway.

Delightful pathways can be made with gravel or granite chippings. Another alternative is the pea gravel which local builders' merchants can often supply. Even mixed ballast from builders' merchants, which is normally used for rough concrete work, can be made into attractive paths. Again, it is important to have a very firm foundation for this type of material, although in this case it is not bedded in concrete or mortar.

If you plan to use crazy paving, the stones should be set in a mortar or concrete bed to prevent them from tipping or moving. Crazy paving is very useful because you can work round curved borders in the herb garden without having to do much cutting or trimming of the stone itself.

You can also buy all sorts of prefabricated paving materials, which are available in a wide range of colours and sizes. Mix the sizes together carefully and you will have an interesting and simple way of providing patterned effects. Go for the warm shades such as the pinks and reds, with an occasional touch of a green or natural stone colour here and there. If you want to spend more money on your paving why not consider the paving which has a natural hewn or chiselled surface? This has a rough-textured face or top which gives the appearance of the paving having been hewn from the natural rock. There are even some more expensive paving slabs available, with exposed aggregate which give delightful textured surfaces.

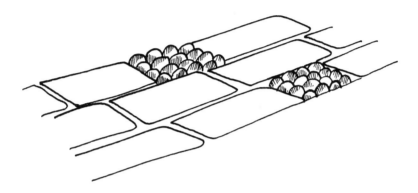

Adding pattern and interest to a paved path. Leave out occasional small slabs and fill in with pebbles.

Another interesting way to make a path with a difference in your herb garden is to use either crazy paving pieces or ordinary slabs but leave out a slab here and there and fill in the site with large pebbles. These form a most unusual pattern, but they must be set in a bed of mortar or cement, so that the tops of the pebbles lie level with the tops of the paving surround. You can easily check the level by placing a straight board across the paving and the tops of the pebbles as work proceeds. You can also make patterns by leaving out slabs here and there, filling in the spaces with some good compost with plenty of organic matter or peat worked in, and then planting one or two creeping herbs so that eventually, when they become established, they will creep and cover over the paths which will look very effective.

Using Walling Units

Walling stones are also available in various colours, various sizes and with textured or natural rough faces. With these walling units you can build up low raised beds in which you can plant your herbs, or you can form single-course edgings to the various beds, so that the garden has a neat appearance. This is a good way of providing a planting site where your soil is of poor quality because you can buy in some good soil from elsewhere, fill up the areas and add extra depth to the soil by a low brick wall surround to the beds.

4

A BASIC RANGE TO GROW

Now comes the really exciting part of the herb story, the actual selection of the different ones to grow. There is of course a bewildering array of fascinating herbs to try, but in this chapter we are looking at the basic herbs, which will be ideal for most culinary requirements.

The herbs recommended are listed in alphabetical order.

Basil
There are in fact three types of Basil. The first one is *Ocymum basilicum*, which is a small plant and is an ideal herb to use with meat, vinegar, cheese, game, and tomatoes. Unfortunately, it is not very hardy, and a slightly hardier type is *O. minimum*, though it is in fact smaller growing. This type is a good choice for the small herb garden, and is generally the best one to grow as it attains a spread and height of not much more than 12 inches (30cm). The Dark Opal Basil, the third kind, has very pretty bronze leaves and is an excellent plant for window boxes.

Basil is a half-hardy annual and it should be grown in a sheltered part of the herb garden with plenty of sunlight. A light type of soil is best for it. Seed should be sown in early April in a greenhouse or a frame, and when the seedlings are large enough to handle they should be pricked out into deeper boxes and finally, in order to encourage really good roots, potted up singly in 3-inch (7cm) pots. Again, you should select a good potting compost for the sowing and potting sequence.

The small plants must be hardened off carefully before they are planted out finally in their permanent quarters. A spacing of about 12 inches (30cm) each way is necessary if you are growing more than one clump of plants. Usually, the planting time will be around the first or second week in June. If you feel lazy you can sow the seed where the plants are to grow, carrying this work out in late April. It is important to sow as thinly as possible, and you will still have to thin carefully as soon as the plants are large enough to handle.

Basil

Borage (*Borago officinalis*)
This is a delightful herb with an unusual mild cucumber flavour.
It is excellent for use in salads and summer drinks such as cider
cups and Pimms cups. It grows 2 or 3 feet (60cm-1m) high in
good soil, though in slightly poorer conditions it may only reach
a height of some 18 inches (45cm). Bees love this herb with its
attractive blue flowers.

Borage

Borage is a hardy annual which needs a sunny and sheltered
position. It may grow in light shade, but must not be planted
where it is very shady. Fortunately, it is a plant which is not too
fussy about its soil and one can safely say that it will grow in
any reasonable soil conditions.

Seeds should be sown where the plants are to grow out in the
garden, in April. Sow as thinly as possible and thin out later to a
final spacing of about 12 inches (30cm) apart. Borage will shed
its seeds naturally and you will find that lots of nice little new
seedlings will pop up around the base of the parent plants.

Chervil (*Anthriscus cerefolium*)
This is a delightfully easy herb to grow and by making frequent sowings you can have pickings for most of the season. It is ideal for garnishing in place of Parsley, and is also used in soups. Incidentally, the herb makes new potatoes even more delicious. It is a hardy annual, growing to about 12 inches (30cm) high and 15-18 inches (37-45cm) across.

Chervil should be grown in a warm, sunny situation but it is not too fussy about its soil. The sowing period can be quite an extensive one, starting in early March and going through to the late autumn, somewhere around the end of September. Seed can be sown where the plants are to grow, and again should be sown as thinly as possible and thinned out as soon as the seedlings can be handled. Seeds should be sown some $\frac{1}{4}$ inch deep (6mm) and the seedlings should be thinned to about 12 inches apart (30cm). In order to provide a continuity of picking, it is a good plan to sow once every four to five weeks if you have the room. The early and late sowings should really be protected by glass, either in the greenhouse or in the cold frame.

Chervil

Chives

This is the really easy way to provide some delicate onion flavouring without having to grow onions or salad onions. There are three types of Chive. The first one is the popular onion, *Allium schoenoprasum*, which is the kind we are all familiar with. It has thin tubular foliage and grows about 8 inches (20cm) high and forms little compact bushes some 10 inches (25cm) in diameter.

There is a giant Chive, which is ideal for cutting for larger amounts, and an attractive, ornamental one, the Chinese version, *Allium tuberosum*. Both these grow to a height of some 12 inches (30cm), and have a slightly stronger flavour than the first kind.

Chives

Chives are very useful ingredients of the herb garden because they are perennial plants, which means that they are there every year. They can be grown in full sunlight. A little care with soil is important for really good leafy growth, and good drainage and plenty of organic matter are two important points to bear in mind. Seed can be sown from April to September where the plants are to grow, sowing about ½ inch (1cm) deep. Later, thin the seedlings to about 6 inches (15cm) apart, and 12 inches (30cm) for the larger types of Chive. About six months after you have sown the seed you should have plants that are ready for use.

Eventually, the Chives will make quite large clumps and it will be necessary to divide them up in order to give them more growing room. This can be done approximately every four years and the extra clumps can be planted out elsewhere to increase your Chive plants.

Garlic (*Allium sativum*)

What would the herb garden be without some garlic? This is a very potent herb and only the slightest touch is needed to add

Garlic

delicious flavouring to salads, and all sorts of dishes. It is grown by its cloves or little bulbs, and such is the strength of the clove flavour, that it is only necessary to wipe round the salad bowl in order to provide the flavour. Garlic is ideal for flavouring meat, vegetable dishes, soups and stews.

It is a perennial plant and grows to a maximum height of 2 feet (60cm) but usually only to about 12-18 inches (30-45cm). The clumps can spread about 12 inches (30cm) across in good conditions. It must have full sunlight in order to grow and ripen well, and the best soil is one which is extremely well drained, and preferably light.

The cloves or little bulblets are planted in early March, with each one 6 inches (15cm) apart in rows about 12-15 inches (30-37cm) apart. The cloves are pressed into the soil so that they are just covered. It is a good plan to keep an eye on the new planting because early frosts can lift the cloves out of the ground and they may need pressing back again every so often until they have taken root well.

Horseradish (*Armoracia rusticana*)

Horseradish has a bad name amongst many gardeners because it is a rather invasive type of plant. It has long tap roots, at least 12-18 inches (30-45cm) long, and if pieces are left in the ground they quickly take root. It is as well, therefore, to keep a careful eye on any plantings of this very useful herb. It grows to a height of about 2 feet (60cm), has a spread of some 15 inches (37cm), and is a perennial plant. Grated horseradish makes the well-known sauce that is so superb with roast beef. It can also be used for fish dishes.

To grow really well, it must have a deeply worked soil so that you get as long a root as possible, and deep digging to a depth of at least 15 inches (37cm) is important. Under no circumstances should the soil have fresh manure incorporated; keep to the composted vegetable waste or the peats. The situation can be in the full sun or light shade, and Horseradish is planted out during

Horseradish

the middle of March, planting about 12 inches (30cm) apart and just covering the tops with soil. It is very easily propagated because you only need small pieces of root when lifting the mature plants at the end of the season, and these little roots can be planted out to make up new beds or plantations.

Marjoram
There are two main types of interest; the pot Marjoram, *Origanum onites*, and the sweet Marjoram, *O. marjorana*. How do you decide which to grow? The answer is simple – if you like more bitter flavour to your Marjoram, then you should grow the pot type, but if you require a more delicate and sweeter flavour, then the sweet Marjoram is the one for you. The first type is a perennial and has a height and spread of between 12 and 15 inches (30-37cm). It likes a sheltered situation and needs plenty

of sunlight, too. The soil must be well dug over and well enriched, and the plant can be raised from seed sown in the spring or the autumn. Seed is sown where the plants are to grow, sowing in $\frac{1}{4}$-inch (6mm) deep drills, spacing the drills about 12 inches (30cm) apart if a lot of the plants are to be grown. Thin later on when the seedlings are easy to handle, to about 12 inches (30cm) apart. You can buy pot-grown plants and these are generally planted out in March or April.

Marjoram

The sweet Marjoram is a half hardy annual growing much taller, to a height of at least $1\frac{1}{2}$-2 feet (45-60cm) and has quite a spread of some 12 to 15 inches (30-37cm). It needs plenty of sunlight and must have a well drained and enriched soil.

The plants are raised from seed, sowing outdoors in late April, $\frac{1}{4}$-inch (6mm) deep, and thinning later to 12 inches (30cm) apart. Alternatively, you can make a slightly earlier start under glass in the frames or the greenhouse, sowing in a good compost, pricking out later on, and finally potting up in 3-inch (7cm) pots, hardening off and planting out in early June, 12 inches (30cm) apart.

Mint

There are several types of Mint which you can grow in your herb garden. There is the popular Spearmint or Garden Mint, *Mentha viridis*. This grows about 15 inches (37cm) high and is ideal for mint sauce. Another type is Apple Mint, *M. rotundifolia variegata*. This is a much taller plant, growing at least $1\frac{1}{2}$-2 feet (45-60cm) high, with a very nice apple flavour. Many people prefer it to the more well-known one. Probably the best flavoured mint is *M. rotundifolia*. This is known as Bowles Mint, named after the raiser. It too grows about $1\frac{1}{2}$-2 feet (45-60cm) high.

Mint

Mint is a perennial plant which likes a partly shaded situation, although it will do quite well in a very sunny locality. It is important to provide a moist soil, and this can be achieved by working in plenty of moist peat. Unfortunately, mint spreads very rapidly and needs containing either by placing a row or two of bricks around the planting site below ground level, or even by lining the planting area with some polythene sheeting, punching one or two holes in the bottom for drainage. Another plan of campaign to contain the mint is to lift the clumps every season or so, shaking out all the root systems, and replanting them. In this way the spread of the vigorous roots can be contained quite well.

Mint is planted either in the autumn or in the spring, and all you do is to place pieces of root about 4-6 inches (10-15cm) in length, spaced about 2 inches (5cm) apart, in the bottom of a prepared flat area. Replace the soil firmly and keep well watered. There is no problem about propagating of the plant − it is so invasive that you will find the roots spreading rapidly. However, if you do want to propagate Mint, all you need to do is to lift a few roots, cut them into smaller pieces and replant them elsewhere.

Parsley

Another essential of the herb garden is Parsley. Perhaps the best type of the three available is the French *Carum petroselinum*. It grows about 10 inches (25cm) high and has an exquisite flavour. The leaves, incidentally, are not curled. There is something to be said for having an attractive plant in your herb garden too, so why not include the Curled Parsley. This grows 9 or 10 inches (22-25cm) high and is ideal for sauces and for garnishing.

The plant is a biennial and will spread at least 12 inches (30cm) across when well established. It does need a well dug soil with plenty of good root room, and it must also have moisture. It is advisable to keep a sheltered part of the herb garden for Parsley. It can be propagated by sowing some seed in late March and also in late July for winter and spring harvesting. Seed should be sown as thinly as possible, about $\frac{1}{4}$-inch (6mm) deep, spacing the drills about 12 inches (30cm) apart if you want more than one row.

Parsley

Another idea is to sow seed over a small patch, making sure that the sowing is made as thinly and as evenly as possible. Later on, any seed which has been sown will have to have its seedlings thinned out to about 10 inches (25cm) apart each way.

It is a good plan to give some protection for winter plants by placing a cloche or two over the clumps, making sure that the ends to the cloches are sealed.

Rosemary

Another popular and easy to grow herb is Rosemary, *Rosmarinus officinalis*. It is an evergreen shrub, growing to a height of about 4 feet (1.3m), which will spread 3-5 feet (1-1.6m) wide, according to the vigour of its growth. Rosemary is a useful subject to include in your herb garden because it gives height and character to the layout, and you can also use one or two of the shrubs as a very attractive and practical windbreak. It has pretty blue flowers which appear in April. The herb is used for game, stews, lamb, and also for herb butter and even some soups. Rosemary flowers can be used to make a fragrant garnish for a fruit cup.

Rosemary

Select a sunny and reasonably sheltered situation. The soil should be deeply dug and preferably on the light side. You can buy plants to plant out in April or you can sow seeds in March in a seed box in a frame or in the open in drills about $\frac{1}{4}$-inch (6mm) deep. When finally planted out the young plants should be at least 3 feet (1m) apart each way if several are to be grown.

Sage

This is another must for the basic herb garden. There are two types, the narrow-leaved Sage, which grows to a height of 2-2$\frac{1}{2}$ feet (60-75cm), and *Salvia officinalis*. The former type is better to grow, however, because it is slightly hardier.

Sage, a very useful herb to use with onions for stuffing, is a shrub growing to a height of about 2 feet (60cm) which will spread to a similar measurement. It is versatile because it will grow either in a very sunny situation or in partial shade. It is important to appreciate, though, that a warm site is very important if the oils in the leaves which make its flavour are to be encouraged to mature or develop. This only happens in a

Sage

warm situation. Select a well drained bed for the plant, and a lighter type of soil is best. You can buy plants from your local garden centre or nursery, or seed can be sown in April and the seedlings can be thinned out to about 12 inches (30cm) apart each way. Unfortunately, Sage goes off, as it were, when the plant becomes older so it is a good plan to raise some fresh plants every two seasons or so.

Tarragon
There are two types of Tarragon, the French and the Russian, of which the French has the better flavour, though it is

unfortunately not quite so hardy as the Russian. It is excellent for making Tarragon vinegar, and for omelette flavouring, sauces, soups, and so on. It is a hardy perennial plant, growing some 2 feet (60cm) high and spreading about 14-18 inches (35-45cm) wide, and so it is a useful herb for giving an extra bit of height in the herb garden layout. A sheltered site is important; under no circumstances must the plants be exposed to very hard weather conditions as they could be killed off during severe winters. The soil must be well drained, so if it is on the heavy side you may have to omit Tarragon from your garden unless you can prepare the ground by incorporating plenty of gritty material or compost in order to ensure open and well drained soil.

Tarragon

You can buy plants from your local nursery or garden centre and planting can take place in the late autumn, in late September, or in mid-March. Planting distances are about 18 inches (45cm) apart each way. The number of plants can be increased quite easily by dividing them in March or early April.

Thyme

There are two different kinds of Thyme. One is the common or popular Thyme, *Thymus vulgaris*, which grows to about 12 inches (30cm) high. The other type is the Lemon Thyme, *T. citrovis*. This is slightly dwarfer, growing to 9 or 10 inches (22-25cm) in height. Both Thymes are ideal for flavouring stuffings, soups and stews. They are shrubby plants and require an open and warm, sunny situation. They are not too fussy about their soil, but they do like a site which is well drained. The plants can be raised from seed sown in late April in shallow drills, thinning later on to about 12 inches (30cm) apart. Plants can also be obtained from a local source, and planting can take place in late March or in the autumn, in late September or early October.

Thyme

The plant does become weak when it gets older, and it is therefore a good plan to remake the bed every three seasons or so. This can be done by lifting and dividing the established plants in April.

This concludes the suggestions for the popular and easy to grow herbs for your herb garden. Grouped together, all these herbs will provide you with a very attractive layout, both in formation of foliage and also in variation of height and spread. Those included which are of quite a reasonable height give extra character to the layout, a very important point when planning your herb garden.

All these herbs will not take up a great deal of room, but you can of course make your own personal selection and double up the numbers wherever necessary, or reduce the different types which are grown. Many of the smaller herbs mentioned will be ideal for container planting in tubs or in a window box, in which case do bear in mind that it is important to work plenty of organic matter into your soil when doing the initial preparations; this keeps the plants growing well and prevents any distress or dying back of the growth due to dryness of the roots. Remember that an extremely hot dry summer can cause problems unless this sponge material has been put in so that the soil retains valuable moisture.

5

A MORE AMBITIOUS RANGE OF HERBS

After the more common or garden herbs, widely used in the culinary and medicinal arts, come the less known and little used plants. Some of them are almost forgotten, except in large, old-fashioned herb gardens where they bloom unseen for most of the year. They are well worth cultivating, even just two or three choice specimens. We have sub-divided them into culinary, fragrant and old-fashioned, and medicinal herbs. Some of the medicinal ones have very historical and legendary powers, and some of the old remedies can be useful today.

CULINARY HERBS
Angelica (*Angelica archangelica*)
This has always been surrounded by superstition, and is considered to have magical and medicinal powers. The name is derived from the Archangel Michael, who is said to have appeared in a vision in the 14th century and claimed that the herb would cure the plague. It is a very large plant, growing to a height of 6-10 feet (2-3.3m), so is suitable for the back of a border or herb garden. As it is a biennial, it dies after producing seeds, but it seeds itself abundantly so that keeping new plants

growing is no problem. The seedlings can be transplanted as soon as they are large enough to handle.

Angelica

Two plants are all that are necessary to provide Angelica for a family. It grows best in rich moist soil, in a sunny or part-shaded position. Sow seed in March to April, $\frac{1}{2}$-inch (12mm) deep in groups of three or four, and about 3 feet (1m) apart in their actual growing position. When the seedlings are large enough, remove all the weak ones, and leave the strongest to grow on. You can sow the seeds in a seed bed or pan in the greenhouse, and transplant the seedlings to their final growing position in the late autumn or following March. These plants may not grow as large as the ones that have been left to grow on in their original position.

The stems can be candied, and the stems and leaves used with apples and rhubarb.

Coriander (*Coriandrum sativum*)
This is a hardy annual herb, grown mainly for its seeds. The Elizabethans were very partial to roast pork rubbed with equal amounts of powdered Coriander and Fennel seeds. The plant is easy to grow and requires little attention. It does best in soil enriched with well-rotted manure or compost in a sunny position. Sow seeds $\frac{1}{4}$-inch (6mm) deep where they are to grow. Thin out the plants to 10 inches (25cm) between each plant as soon as they are large enough to handle. About a dozen plants are needed if seeds are to be used for flavouring. The plants grow to about 18 inches (45cm) high with a spread of 6-9 inches (15-22cm). Before ripening, the seeds have an unpleasant odour, but improve on ripening to a pleasant, spicy odour. These are then ready to be harvested and dried on trays, either in the sun or indoors. On drying, shake out the seeds and store in airtight containers.

Coriander

Fennel (*Foeniculum vulgare*)

There are two varieties of Fennel, the Florence Fennel, grown mainly for its swollen stem base and used as a vegetable, and the perennial herb that is cultivated for its flavourful leaves, stems and seeds. The perennial herb is the one we are talking about here. It has leaves with a delicate aniseed flavour, which enhance fish, sauces, pickles, and cheese dishes. It grows to a height of 5-8 feet (1.6-2.6m) with blue green feathery leaves.

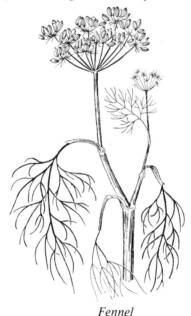

Fennel

Fennel needs a warm, sunny position in well-drained soil. Sow the seeds thinly in March, so that seeds on the plant will have time to ripen in September or October. If grown for leaves and stems, sow in April or May. Three plants would be ample for a supply of seeds, leaves and stems. Thin the plants when large enough, to 12 inches (30cm) apart. Pick the leaves as required from June onwards. To harvest the seeds, gather them on a dry day in early autumn when they have turned pale brown and hang them in a warm place for a week or two, until they are quite dry. Then store in air-tight containers.

Lovage (*Levisticum officinale*)
Lovage is one of the oldest known herbs, believed to have been brought over to this country by the Romans. It was used extensively in the Middle Ages for medicines and for flavouring soups and stews. These days it has almost disappeared, although it was very popular in medieval herb gardens. It resembles a giant celery in shape, and has a similar taste too. It would

Lovage

provide a distinctive feature in any garden. The leaves are mostly used for flavouring, especially in stews and soups, but can also be used sparingly in salads and omelettes. It grows successfully in well-drained soil in a sunny or partially shaded position. Seeds can be sown in September or March, about $\frac{1}{2}$-inch (12mm) deep in the position in which they are to grow. When the seedlings are big enough to handle, thin them to 12 inches (30cm) apart. Two or three plants will be quite enough to provide sufficient fresh and dried leaves for flavouring. During the summer, remove flowering stems to promote the growth of young leaves. To increase your stock, the roots can be divided in March and replanted at 12-inch (30cm) intervals. Pick the leaves during the summer, from June to October.

Savory (Summer – *Satureia hortensis* – and Winter – *Satureia montana*)
These both come from the Mediterranean, but whereas the winter variety is a shrubby, evergreen perennial, the summer one

Savory

is a hardy annual. Both are grown for their spicy-flavoured leaves, which are excellent used with sausages, pork pies and sauces. They prefer well-drained soil in a sunny position. For a summer supply of either variety, sow seeds $\frac{1}{4}$ inch (6mm) deep in April. When large enough to handle, thin them to 6-9 inches (15-22cm) apart. For a winter supply of Summer Savory, sow a few seeds in a seed pan in September. When large enough, prick out into 3-inch (7cm) pots, using potting compost, and grow on either indoors or in the greenhouse in a temperature of 45-50°F (7-10°C). Three or four plants of Summer Savory and one or two of the winter variety should be ample for household needs. As Winter Savory is what we call a 'sub-shrub', its base becomes very woody and plants need to be replaced at intervals of about two to three years.

The leaves of both types can be picked as needed. For drying, the Summer Savory can be picked in August. The leaves and shoots can also be deep frozen.

Sorrel (Broad-leaved – *Rumex acetosa*. French – *Rumex scutatus*)
These two herbs are grown for their leaves, which give a sharp taste to stews and soups. They are both hardy perennials and like deep, moist soil and a sunny position. Sow seed in March or April $\frac{1}{4}$ inch (6mm) deep. Thin young plants to 12 inches (30cm) apart. To harvest the leaves, cut before the flowers open. The leaves can be dried and deep frozen.

FRAGRANT AND OLD FASHIONED HERBS
Artemisia (Southern Wood – *Artemisia abrotanum*)
This is a hardy, semi-evergreen shrub of bushy habit, suitable for growing against a wall or in the border. It is grown for its silver-grey, aromatic, feathery foliage. Dull yellow flowers, in elongated panicles, are borne from July to September. This shrub can be grown in any ordinary, well-drained garden soil in a sunny position. Plant in March or April.

Artemisia

Balm, Golden (*Melissa officinalis aurea*)
This is a very decorative herb which can be used as an herbaceous plant. It has lemon-scented leaves, which can be used fresh for flavouring fruit salads and iced drinks. Dried, the leaves retain their fragrance and are an important ingredient in the making of pot-pourri. The golden-green colour of the leaves sometimes fades as the flowers appear.

Plant Balm in ordinary, well-drained soil, preferably in full sun, or sow seeds where the plants are to grow in late April or early May. Thin seedlings to 12 inches (30cm) apart. Cut plants with variegated foliage back to 6 inches (15cm) above ground level in June to encourage more young shoots. In October, cut all growths back to just about ground level, and protect against frost in the colder areas. Use the leaves fresh all through the summer. Leaves to be dried should preferably be gathered before flowering begins.

Balm

Bergamots (*Monarda didyma*)

These are hardy perennials with aromatic leaves, and can be used in the mixed border as well as the herb garden. The mid-green hairy leaves are sometimes dried and used in tea. The bright scarlet flowers which are 3 inches (7cm) across, attract the bees and butterflies, hence the common name, Bee Balm. As named varieties do not come true from seed, plants from a nursery are a better bargain. Bergamots are best planted in groups of four to six plants. They prefer moist soil in sun or partial shade. Division of the roots is advised every two to three years. The leaves can be dried, but must be gathered before the flowers open. Recommended varieties are Cambridge Scarlet, Snow Maiden and Croftway Pink.

Catmint (*Nepeta mussinii*)
This can be used as an edging plant. It has grey-green leaves with spikes of lavender flowers. Cats love the smell of the crushed leaves, and can be seen rolling blissfully about the clumps, so releasing the scent. This plant can be obtained at any good nursery in March or April, and planted in a sunny or partially shaded position in well drained soil. The flowers bloom from May to September, and should be cut down in the autumn.

Evening Primrose (*Oenothera biennis*)
An excellent biennial plant for the border or back of the herb garden. It bears yellow trumpet-shaped flowers which bloom in the evening with a delicate perfume. It grows to a height of about 3 feet (1m) in ordinary garden soil in a sunny position. Plant from October to April, cut down the perennial species to ground level in autumn. As named varieties do not come true from seed, plants should be obtained from a good nursery.

Hyssop (*Hyssopus officinalis*)
An evergreen plant, which can be used as an edging to a herb border, or even as a low ornamental hedge. Purple-blue flowers are borne from July to September. The leaves have a bitter, minty flavour, and can be used in salads, soups and stuffings. They are also a useful ingredient in pot-pourri. Plant any time between September and March in ordinary garden soil. For hedges, plant at intervals of 9-12 inches (22-30cm). Pinch out the growing points to encourage bushy growth. This is also attractive to butterflies and bees.

Hyssop

Lavender (*Lavendula spica*)

No herb garden, or flower garden, come to that, is complete without a lavender bush or hedge. The dwarf varieties are best for the herb garden, especially for edging. Plant lavender any time between September and March in ordinary garden soil and in a sunny position. For hedging, space plants at 9-12 inches (22-30cm) intervals. Lavenders do tend to grow leggy with age, so the best plan is to replant with new stock after five or six years. They can be pruned back each autumn to keep in shape, but straggly plants can be cut hard back in late March or April to encourage new growth from the base. Established hedges can be clipped to shape during the spring.

Lavender

Three dwarf varieties are Hidcote (*Nana atropurpurea*), which has deep violet, highly scented flowers; White Dwarf (*Nana alba*), which has white flowers and is a good rockery plant; and Pink (*Nana rosea*), which has pink flowers, and is attractive as a foil to the blue varieties. The larger varieties – 2-3 feet (60cm-1m) high – are: Seal, which has long spikes of deep colour, and is excellent for drying; and Old English, the traditional lavender, with purple fragrant flowers. Again, of course, these flowers attract the bees and butterflies.

Lemon Verbena (*Lippia citriodora*)
This delightful plant is a half-hardy deciduous shrub with leaves that have a strong lemon scent when crushed. It grows to a height of 5 feet (1.6m) and has a 4-foot (1.3m) spread, with pale mauve tubular flowers in August. Plant in late May, preferably

against a south facing wall in a sheltered position in full sun. As it is rather tender, it should be protected in winter, especially in the northern and eastern part of the country. You may find that the shrub is cut back by frost, but new growths will appear from the base in spring.

Mezereon (*Daphne mezereum*)

This is a fragrant, hardy deciduous shrub, with spikes of purple pink flowers, very freely produced in February to March. The perfume is very heady and of a lemony, lily of the valley fragrance. This Daphne can be raised from seed, in sandy peaty soil in a sunny position. Plants can be put in in October to November, and March to April. The berries are definitely not edible and children should leave them alone.

Mint (*Mentha*)

When mint is mentioned one automatically thinks of roast lamb with mint sauce, but there are other varieties which can be grown simply for their fragrant leaves. Two such varieties are Citrata (Lemon Mint), which has lemon scented leaves, and Citrata Var (Eau-de-Cologne Mint), which speaks for itself. This variety also has heart-shaped bronze leaves which are most attractive. They need a sunny or partially-shaded site, preferably one that does not dry out in summer. As Mints are notoriously invasive, it is as well to try and restrict them to their own part of the garden by embedding slates or tiles vertically around them. One variety which can be used ornamentally as well as in culinary ways is the Apple Mint, *Mentha rotundifolia*. This is generally considered the best flavoured mint, and has attractive leaves with creamy-white margins.

Rue (*Ruta graveolens*)

This is a hardy evergreen sub-shrub, which has been used as a culinary herb but is now mainly grown as a decorative plant.

Rue

The leaves can be chopped and added sparingly to salads to add a bitter flavour. A good subject for the herbaceous border, or as a low hedge, Rue has blue-green aromatic leaves with clusters of sulphur-yellow flowers borne in June and July. Plant from September to March in a sunny position.

For hedging, plant at 12-inch (30cm) intervals. Prune back in April to the old wood to preserve the bushy shape or to keep the hedging from becoming leggy. Remove the dead flower clusters in autumn.

Squill (*Urginea maritima*)
This is a very ancient herb used medicinally by Pliny and Dioscorides, and the bulb used to be used as a rat poison. It is a half-hardy bulbous plant, with attractive small white flowers. As it is a slightly tender plant, it should be grown in an unheated greenhouse in well-drained pots of light loam and sand.

Spurge Laurel (*Daphne laureola*)
Laurel is an evergreen hardy shrub with dark green shiny leaves, and very fragrant greeny-yellow flowers, borne in February and March, which are followed by black berries in the autumn. The foliage is particularly handsome. The plant grows to a height of 3 feet (1m) and should be planted in September or March and April in ordinary garden soil. It likes a sunny or partially shaded position. No pruning is required, except for cutting out straggly growths in the spring.

Thymes (*Thymus*)
These plants are different varieties from the basic Thymes described in the last chapter. *Thymus fragrantissimum* has the perfume of oranges and balsam, and is also good to use for culinary purposes and pot-pourri. *Thymus citriodorus aureus*, the Golden Lemon Thyme, is lemon-scented with golden leaves which are more apparent in winter. They will grow in any garden soil in an open, sunny position. Cut off the flower heads after flowering to maintain dense, healthy plants. Also under this heading come the creeping Thymes. These are ideal for the herb garden or planted in between paving slabs. Two varieties are *Thymus serpyllum minus*, which has red and white forms and is one of the smallest aromatic plants, and *Thymus* 'Lemon Curd', the scent of which speaks for itself.

MEDICINAL HERBS
Arnica (*Arnica montana*)
Arnica grows to about 2 feet (60cm) high and has orange-yellow daisies growing from the leaf rosette. The extract of the plant is one of the strongest herbal antiseptics. Plant in spring or autumn in ordinary garden soil in a sunny position.

Bistort (*Polygonum bistorta*)
The leaves of Bistort were used in Easter pudding, and also as

an astringent. Mostly used in the herbaceous border where it becomes a mat-forming plant with spikes of pink flowers produced in May and June, with a second crop following in late summer. The variety 'Superbum' is the one most commonly used in cultivation. Plant in October to March in rich moist soil in full sun or partial shade.

Blood Root (*Sanguinaria canadensis*)
The common name is derived from the red sap that comes from the fleshy roots. American Indians used it as a dye. It is an extremely beautiful plant with waxy white flowers and palmate grey green leaves, which grows to a height of 6 inches (15cm). Blood Root grows best in soil containing leaf mould or peat, in a sunny or part-shaded position.

Colchicum (*Colchicum autumnale*)
These attractive flowers grow from corms planted in August or September. Six or more should be planted in groups where they can be seen to their best advantage. The pink, crocus-shaped flowers appear long before the leaves, in the autumn. Colchicum was used externally for gout, as the extract is poisonous.

Comfrey (*Symphytum officinale*)
Comfrey is used to alleviate pain and reduce swelling in breaks and sprains. The roots and leaves, boiled with sugar and lemon added, relieve congestion of the chest. The plant is suitable for moist areas, such as the edges of streams or pools. It has rough, hairy leaves with bell-shaped or tubular blue flowers.

Note: Pending further investigations following warnings from Australia that an alkaloid present in Comfrey may cause liver damage leading to liver cancer authorities in the U.K. recommend that Comfrey is not taken internally in any form.

Foxglove (*Digitalis purpurea*)

This well-known plant is used as a heart stimulant. There are many varieties of this plant, one of which is 'Foxy' which grows to only 3 feet (1m). They are best grown as biennials as they tend to deteriorate after the second year. Plant between October and April in ordinary garden soil in partial shade, making sure that the site does not dry out in summer.

Herb Paris (*Paris quadrilolia* – Herb True Love)

A plant which, according to folk lore, is owned by Venus, Herb Paris bears a four-petalled yellow-green flower with four pointed leaves. All these are surmounted by a purplish-black berry. It is a hardy perennial, with a rhyzome root, like the Iris, and prefers sandy soil and a shady situation. Seeds can be sown outdoors in the autumn, and plants in October or March. It reaches a height of 6 inches (15cm). Medicinally, it is used as an antidote to poisons.

Horehound (*Marrubium vulgare*)

This is a hardy perennial medicinal herb, the leaves and shoots of which are used as a popular remedy for coughs and colds. It grows 1-2 feet (30-60cm) high, with grey velvety leaves and white flowers borne in June to September. Plants can be grown in March or April in ordinary garden soil, and seeds can be sown in a shady position outdoors from March to May. Alternatively, cuttings can be put in a shady position in April.

Lobelia (*Lobelia syphilitica*)

A half-hardy perennial, this herb is used medicinally as an emetic and for chest complaints, and was first introduced into Britain in the 17th century. It likes a sunny position in ordinary garden soil in June until October, when the plants must be lifted and placed in pots in the greenhouse to furnish cuttings for the following spring. Cut off the flower stems about two weeks before lifting. The flowers are a most attractive blue shade.

Marshmallow (*Althaea officinalis* – Mortification Plant)
The Ancient English name comes from a soothing lotion made from the leaves and flowers, and the root yields soothing mucilage. It has soft velvety grey leaves with rose-pink flowers, and is a hardy perennial. Ordinary garden soil is its natural habitat in a sunny aspect, and it grows to a height of 3 feet (1m). The dried root can be used to make Marshmallow sweets.

Mullein (*Verbascum thapsus*)
Mullein is the herb of the Irish Patron Saint of Gardeners, St Fiacre. It is a biennial herb, growing 4-8 feet (1.3-2.6m) tall with clusters of marginally toothed leaves covered with white woolly hairs and spikes of yellow flowers borne from June to August. Verbascums like full sun and ordinary garden soil. Plant in October, or March to April. If grown in exposed positions, the plants may require staking. In November, cut down to ground level.

Orris (*Iris florentina*)
The powdered root of this plant was used by ladies of the 18th century as face powder, because it smells of violets. It is one of the Intermediate Bearded Irises with a pale blue and white flower. Orris likes a sunny border and ordinary garden soil. Plant in July, October or March, keeping the rhyzomes or roots near the surface. As it reproduces itself each year and forms great clumps, it is a good plan to lift and replant every fourth year, and so divide the rhyzomes.

Samphire (*Crithmum maritimum*)
This hardy perennial herb grows mostly near the sea shore. The leaves are used for pickling, and the plant has thick fleshy stalks with tufts of white flowers. It prefers a sandy soil and shady position, and is not easy to grow away from the sea.

Scullcap (*Scutellaria laterifolia*)
Scullcap is a hardy perennial, with blue trumpet-like flowers, hence the name, Scullcap or Helmet flower. It is used to soothe headaches and grows to a height of 2 feet (60cm). The plant thrives in full sun or partial shade, and should be planted between September and March in ordinary garden soil; it is ideal for rock gardens. Seeds can be sown under glass in March or April, and planted outdoors in September. The plants need to be cut back in February within 4 inches (10cm) of the base. During growth in the spring stop the main shoots once or twice to encourage a bushy habit. Divide and replant only when overgrown.

Self-Heal (*Prunella vulgaris*)
This is a very 'showy' hardy perennial plant, suitable for herb gardens and rock gardens. It grows to a height of 8 inches (20cm) with frilly cut leaves and violet flowers. As its name suggests, it was used as a healing herb. Plant in ordinary garden soil in March, in sun or partial shade. It is a good idea to 'dead head' the plants regularly during the summer, so as to avoid the growth of seedlings which can become a nuisance. Also, this plant needs to be kept within bounds as it tends to become invasive.

Tansy (*Tanacetum vulgare*)
A herb very commonly used in the 16th and 17th centuries, but almost forgotten today, Tansy has very aromatic leaves which were used for flavouring puddings and cakes, and for garnishing. It is a hardy perennial with silvery foliage and yellow flowers, borne in dense clusters in August. The herb is very easy to grow and likes gritty soil in a sunny position. Plant in March, and remove the dead flower stems during the summer and autumn. Re-plant every three to four years.

Valerian (*Valeriana officinalis*)
This is a hardy perennial herb, used as a pain killer and for promoting sleep. It grows to a height of 3 feet (1m) and has tiny pink flowers with a strong perfume. Plant from October to March, with a light staking in March if the plants are grown in exposed conditions. A little rhyme, coming from the North in the seventeenth century, goes as follows:

> 'They that will have their heale
> Must put Setwell in their Keale.'

'Keale' is another word for meal.

Wood Sorrel (*Oxalis acetosella*)
This is a hardy perennial, which naturalizes well in shady corners where it will seed freely. It forms tufts of pale green heart-shaped leaves and bears pearl-white flowers from March to May. This herb is used in salads and has a sharp taste. Plant in March or September.

Yarrow (*Achillea millefolium*)
A hardy perennial growing to a height of 2 feet (60cm) with fine-cut deep green leaves, and white scented flowers, which appear from June to September. Plant between October and March in ordinary garden soil in a sunny position. Cut back to ground level in November. Yarrow tea was an excellent remedy for severe colds.

6

THE GENERAL CARE OF HERBS

The amount of care or management your herb garden will require will depend to a very great extent on the condition of the site initially. If your garden is a new one and built up from scratch, then you are bound to be faced with more than the usual amount of weeds and weed seedlings and this means that you will have a little more work initially. If, on the other hand, you have been lucky enough to take over an established garden, the weed problem will be minimal. It is important, especially with the newer gardens, to keep those weeds down, because there will be competition between the weed growth and the establishment of your new herb plants. Under no circumstances should you allow the weeds to take over; they will dwarf the other plants and, what is more important, they will take away valuable food nutrients and moisture.

The aim in basic care, is to keep the hoe going regularly throughout the season, killing off the seedling weeds as soon as they appear above the surface of the ground. This regular hoeing has another benefit. It prevents the surface becoming caked or hardened and this stirring helps to aerate the soil. All plant roots must breathe and it is important that the air can get down into the root area.

In the more established herb garden it may be a little difficult to hoe easily with the long handled Dutch hoe, but the small hand hoe or the old fashioned onion hoe is ideal for this purpose. In fact, many of our leading tool manufacturers these days produce some delightful little hand tools, especially the hand hoes. These are useful for working in between the clumps of the plants, loosening the soil and getting rid of persistent weeds. Of course, there may be the odd weed which escapes the eye initially, but as soon as it is noticed it should be carefully pulled up by hand.

It is a good plan to keep an eye on some of the taller types of herbs and give them a little support with twiggy pieces of stick in their early stages. Some of the tall herbs can be kept neat and tidy by placing one or more canes close by them, taking care that when the canes are inserted in the soil that the roots are not damaged. Once these canes are firmly in position, a few ties around the plant and around the canes will encircle the plant and keep the foliage neat and trim. This training or tying of the taller plants is important in gardens which are a little exposed. Strong winds can loosen plants and as a result they never become happily established.

Feeding the Plants
The plants will require a little feeding occasionally, though your initial soil preparations should have been thorough enough to give your plants a really good start. You will have to think ahead to future seasons and your aim must be to maintain strong healthy growth. There are two ways in which you can feed your herb borders. You can use a dry or granular feed which is carefully scattered in between the clumps at rates not exceeding $1-1\frac{1}{2}$ oz (25-37g) per square yard/metre. Ideally, this should be done during showery weather so the fertilizer is washed into the

soil. In any case, it is always a good plan to hoe lightly in between the plants so that the fertilizer is well worked into the top soil.

You can also apply a liquid fertilizer – this is a concentrated feed which is diluted in water and then applied with a watering can. This method ensures that the feed gets down to the plants roots even more quickly. The same sort of feed can be used as a folia or leaf feed. Many of the leafier, fleshier plants will assimilate this food very quickly through their stems and leaves, and this is the quickest way to provide a tonic for them.

Although a fertilizer such as sulphate of ammonia can encourage rapid green growth, it should be used very sparingly because (a) it can burn plants if applied carelessly, and (b) over-feeding with it can produce rather weak fleshy leaf growth. It is far better, therefore, to use what is known as a general or well-balanced fertilizer, which contains the essential main plant foods, such as nitrogen, phosphates and potash.

Watering
Never apply fertilizers during dry weather and always make sure that the ground is damp before application, even if it means giving a light spray with the hose pipe or watering can beforehand. It is a good idea, especially on a new herb border, to apply a mulch. This can either be in the form of moist horticultural peat or rotted material from your compost bin. A layer of $\frac{1}{2}$ inch (1cm), and preferably more, around the plants and between them will help you conserve valuable soil moisture in dry weather and will also help to suppress young weed seedlings.

Once the plants have got established, they do not need watering, except of course in exceptionally hot, dry weather when they are showing obvious signs of distress such as flagging or flopping over of the foliage. It is interesting to note that the trickier and tougher plants with aromatic foliage, like Thyme or

Sage, can withstand dry periods much better than their more fleshy or more leafy neighbours. Remember, too, that lack of care and attention to watering can reduce the flavour of many of your herbs.

Watering is especially important where you are growing herbs in containers such as window boxes, tubs or large pots. These always tend to dry out much more rapidly than plants in ordinary beds where there is much greater depth and spread of soil. Despite the fact that the compost for the containers contains a higher proportion of humus material or compost, it is nevertheless vital to keep a special eye on watering these containers so that the soil is kept just nicely moist at all times.

You will find that if containers are placed where they catch a lot of wind, this will dry up the soil very rapidly indeed, so do keep a particularly careful eye on them then.

Fortunately there are very few pests or diseases which attack herbs, but you may occasionally find one or two plants affected by aphids or greenfly. All the anti-greenfly sprays or dusts are very effective, and they should be used strictly in accordance with the makers' instructions on the container or packet. Do bear in mind, though, that the aphid family can multiply very rapidly indeed and unless you keep a careful eye on early infestations it is possible for plants to become really badly affected should you miss out on your spraying. You will find that aphid attack is generally more prevalent during warm, dry weather.

Pruning

The only other attention to detail as far as management is concerned is to keep some plants in check. This means that if you have a confined herb garden it may be necessary, in time, to trim back or clip back some of the more vigorous of the herbs. Plants which are allowed to trail over the edges or across the path edges will have to be cut back so that they do not encroach too much. In many cases this cutting back, which can be done in the summer, will encourage bushier and thicker growth because what you have really done is to prune your plants.

Keep an eye on plants which have been established for several seasons. Some may tend to start dying back, in which case, as you will find in the detailed instructions for individual plants, you must have some stand-by new plants ready to take their place when the older, worn out herbs have been pulled up and discarded. Where there are branches or portions of plants to tie back, or damaged stems, these should be cut out cleanly with a sharp pair of secateurs right down to where new growth arises.

Finally, do not forget to make sure that the labels on your plants are kept easily identifiable, and make sure that none are missing. It is easy to forget the particular variety of a plant if the label gets lost, so it is also a good plan to keep the layout of your herb garden somewhere safe so that, if the labels do get lost you can always identify a clump in a certain position.

7

HARVESTING AND DRYING HERBS

Herbs are best gathered before they flower, as that is when the flavour is at its prime. Try to pick them as soon as the dew has dried and before the sun has become too hot. The leaves must be as dry as possible. This only applies to the annual or deciduous perennials, as evergreen herbs such as Bay, Rosemary and Thyme, can be picked fresh at any time of the year, and do not need to be preserved.

Picking

It is usually the leaves of the plant that are used in flavouring, so these should be picked while young, from early to mid-summer, before they become too tough. Warm, dry days are best for harvesting, preferably using the mornings for picking, before the sun scorches the leaves. As the harvesting process is quite lengthy, it is advisable to pick one variety of herb at a time, especially when dealing with the smaller ones. Pick them as you would flowers, but examine each stem or branch carefully and pull off any damaged or diseased leaves. Tie them into small bunches and dip in boiling water for a few seconds. This preserves their colour, as well as disposing of any insect life still reposing in the foliage. Shake off the excess moisture and leave to dry on absorbent kitchen paper. Large-leaved herbs, such as Sage, Mint and Parsley, can have their leaves stripped from the stalk, but leave small and feathery herbs, such as Fennel and Chervil, on the stalk until drying is completed.

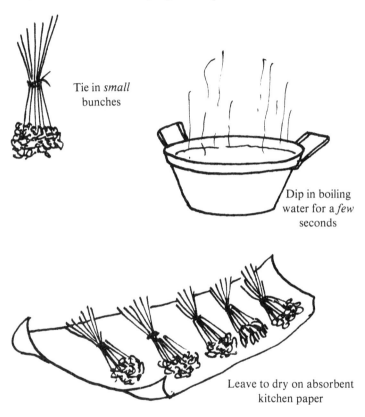

Tie in *small* bunches

Dip in boiling water for a *few* seconds

Leave to dry on absorbent kitchen paper

Preparing herbs for storage.

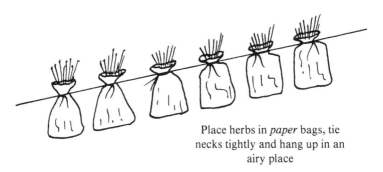

Place herbs in *paper* bags, tie
necks tightly and hang up in an
airy place

Paper bag method.

Drying
To dry herbs successfully, it is essential to have somewhere
where there is abundant dry fresh air, rather than heat. A well-
ventilated larder or garden shed is suitable or, failing that, an
airing cupboard. As a last resort they can be dried in a cool
oven. To dry herbs naturally, put the bunches, leaves down, into
paper bags, binding the top with string or sellotape so that they
are completely encased with only the stalks protruding, and
hang them up in an airy place such as the larder or garden shed.
Do not use plastic bags as these will retain moisture and make
the leaves go mouldy. It will take seven to ten days, according to
the size of the branches or stalks and the humidity of the storage
place, for the herbs to dry completely.

If you have plenty of storage space, drying can be carried out
by placing the herbs, well spaced out, on a tray and putting the
tray in the airing cupboard, over a radiator or even in the
warming drawer of the cooker. Make sure that the leaves or
stalks are turned frequently to ensure even drying. These should
be dry in two to three days.

For the oven method of drying herbs, place the blanched leaves on a muslin or greaseproof paper covered baking tray, well spaced out, and put them into the oven set to the lowest possible temperature. Leave the oven door ajar to allow the moisture to escape. Leave for about 30 minutes, and then turn the leaves over to ensure even drying. The drying process will be completed after about an hour. Turn off the heat, and leave in the oven until they are quite cool. Sage, Mint and Parsley are suitable herbs for this method.

Store in screw-top jars.

Storing

After the herbs are completely dry, crumble them through your fingers, discarding the leaf stalks and midribs. If you want them finer, rub them through a coarse sieve. Store in air tight containers, preferably of pottery or opaque glass. If glass or plastic containers are used, make sure they are stored in a dark place so that the herbs do not lose their colour. It is a good idea to prepare a number of bouquets garni, (one sprig of Parsley, one of Thyme, and a Bay leaf tied in a muslin bag) and store them in an airtight, screw-top jar, to use for flavouring stews, casseroles, soups, and sauces.

Freezing
Another method of preserving herbs is by freezing them. As a rule, you should only freeze those herbs that you are likely to use most, such as Basil, Chives, Mint, Parsley, and Tarragon, because they only have a storage life of six months. Use them to flavour soups and stews by simply crumbling them, still frozen, into the dish to be cooked – there is no need to thaw them first. Indeed, since they become limp when thawed, they are not suitable for garnishing. There is no necessity to blanch herbs before freezing. Pick them fresh from the garden, and keep them separate from each other to prevent them imparting their flavours to one another. Wash and dry thoroughly. Divide into sprigs and pack into polythene bags. All herbs should be wrapped and sealed carefully to prevent other foods in the freezer taking up their scent or flavour. As an extra precaution, put the packs of herbs into a plastic container with a tight-fitting lid.

You can also trim the leaves from the stems, chop finely and put into ice cube trays filled with water. When frozen, wrap each cube in foil and pack into polythene bags in convenient portions. Use the cubes for flavouring while still frozen. You will find that the colour remains good, but the flavour is not strong.

8

COOKING WITH HERBS

Herbs, as we have seen, have been used through the centuries to stimulate the appetite and liven up cooking. Today, with inflation and tight budgeting, they have a practical use too, for it is surprising what delectable dishes can be made with the cheaper cuts of meat by using one or more herbs in the cooking. It is worth remembering, though, that herbs should bring out the best in food and provide a subtle flavour, not swamp the taste of the other ingredients. The golden rule is that herbs used with hot dishes are usually added before cooking is complete, but are put in with the other ingredients in cold and uncooked dishes, so that the flavour can be brought out.

Do not chop or pound fresh herbs; snip them several times with scissors, so that the essence is retained. This is particularly important when using them to spike up salads and omelettes. Unless you are completely *au fait* with using and blending herbs, it is far better to underestimate the amount to be included than to overdo it. Remember, some herbs, like Sage and Bay, are quite strong, so use them particularly sparingly at first.

The following recipes are, in the main, unusual and are worth trying:

SOUPS
Sorrel Soup

$\frac{1}{2}$ lb sorrel leaves
1 onion
1 oz (25g) butter
salt and pepper
$\frac{1}{4}$ lb (100g) lettuce, spinach or turnip tops
$\frac{1}{2}$ lb (225g) potatoes
1 qt (1l) stock or water
$\frac{1}{4}$ pt (150ml) cream (optional)

Shred the leaves, chop the onion and slice the potatoes. Melt the butter in a deep pan and gently fry the leaves, onion and potatoes for 10 minutes. Boil the stock and pour over the vegetables. Simmer for 10-15 minutes. Rub through a sieve, season and re-heat. Add cream just before serving. Sorrel tastes rather like spinach.

Bonne Femme Soup

$\frac{1}{2}$ lettuce
1$\frac{1}{2}$-inch (37mm) length cucumber
1 qt (1l) stock
$\frac{1}{4}$ pt (150ml) milk
lemon juice
$\frac{1}{8}$ pt (50ml) cream
a few leaves of sorrel, chervil, watercress or tarragon
$\frac{1}{2}$ oz (12g) butter
$\frac{1}{2}$ oz (12g) flour
salt and pepper
2 egg yolks

Shred the lettuce and other leaves finely. Cut the cucumber into match-like strips. Melt the butter in a deep pan and fry the vegetables gently for 3 minutes. Add the boiling stock and simmer for 10 minutes. Blend the flour with half the milk, stir this into the soup and cook until it thickens. Season, and add lemon juice to taste. Mix the remaining milk with the egg yolks and cream, add to the soup and cook until the egg yolks thicken, but do not allow to boil. Serve at once.

SAUCES

Everyone knows those familiar white sauces flavoured with herbs, Parsley and bread sauce, but here are a few more sauces using fresh herbs.

Green Sauce

2 or 3 slices of shallot
a handful of parsley
a bunch of watercress
a sprig each of tarragon and fennel
salt and pepper
1 oz (25g) margarine
1 oz (25g) flour
$\frac{1}{2}$ pt (275ml) milk or milk and stock
small glass of white wine (optional)

Blanch the herbs and watercress in boiling water for 1 minute, and plunge them straight into cold water. Drain and rub through a fine sieve. Prepare a white sauce with margarine, flour, seasoning, milk. Add the herbs and wine. Rub through a fine strainer. Re-heat before serving. This can be used with fish, vegetables or poultry.

Fennel Sauce

$\frac{1}{2}$ pt (275ml) white sauce
lemon juice
1 tablespoonful green fennel, chopped

Plunge the fennel into boiling water, drain, chop and add to the sauce. Add a few drops of lemon juice to taste. This is good with fish, especially mackerel.

Sorrel Sauce

½ pt (275ml) white sauce
a good handful of sorrel leaves
salt and pepper
½ oz (12g) butter
nutmeg
2 tablespoonsful cream or top of the milk

Shred the sorrel leaves and cook gently in the butter. Rub through a fine sieve. Bring the white sauce to the boil and whisk in the sorrel *purée*. Season and add a pinch of nutmeg. Stir in cream or top of the milk, but do not re-boil. Use with fish or poultry; or with goose, leaving out the cream.

Cambridge Sauce (cold)

3 hard-boiled eggs
¼ pt (150ml) olive oil
vinegar
½ teaspoonful French mustard
½ teaspoonful chopped capers
1 or 2 chopped anchovies
1 teaspoonful chopped chervil
1 teaspoonful chopped parsley
½ teaspoonful chopped tarragon
½ teaspoonful chopped chives
salt
cayenne pepper

Pound the eggs until smooth, beat in the olive oil, drop by drop, and add enough vinegar to make a thin cream. Blend all the other ingredients into this creamy mixture. Use with salads, fish and cold meats.

Under this heading also comes the savoury vinegars and store sauces. The following are two of the most popular:

Mint Vinegar or Bottled Mint Sauce

1 pt (575ml) wine vinegar
¼ pt (150ml) chopped mint
1 oz (25g) sugar

The mint should be young and fresh. Dry the leaves completely before chopping them, and then add to the vinegar and sugar. This can be strained and used for salad dressings, or left as mint sauce to go with lamb. It will keep throughout the winter months.

Tarragon Vinegar

1 pt (575ml) vinegar
2 oz (50g) tarragon leaves

Bruise the leaves slightly, put into a bottling jar and pour on the vinegar. Screw down the cap and leave for 6 weeks. Strain and rebottle, and store in a cool dry place. If using fresh tarragon, harvest the leaves on a dry day about the end of July, before the flowers appear.

SALADS
Herbs added to salads, either as a garnish or to impart a sharp, unusual taste, can completely change their character. Chervil, basil, marjoram, hyssop, savory, and borage can all be used to great advantage in salads.

An Hors d'oeuvre
Slice an aubergine in thin slices. Soak for 20 minutes in a marinade made from 2 tablespoonsful olive oil, 1 level tablespoonful chopped chives, and 1 level dessertspoonful finely chopped parsley. Drain well and grill slowly. Arrange with the rings slightly overlapping, sprinkle with chopped chives and a little French dressing. Grill for a few minutes until the chives are slightly frizzled. Serve cold.

Salad Bonne Femme

1 bunch watercress
3 cooked potatoes
1 cooked beetroot
4 tomatoes
1 tablespoonful cooked peas
1 teaspoonful chopped parsley
$\frac{1}{4}$ teaspoonful chopped lemon mint
1 teaspoonful anchovy essence

Wash the watercress, dice the potatoes and beetroot, cut the tomatoes into small wedges. Mix lightly together with the herbs and anchovy essence and serve.

Orange Salad

4 sweet oranges
$\frac{1}{2}$ teaspoonful castor sugar
chopped tarragon, chervil and mint
1 tablespoonful French dressing

Peel oranges and discard all pith, cut out the natural orange sections, and sprinkle with sugar. Place in a salad bowl, pour the dressing over and sprinkle with the herbs.

FISH DISHES

Fish can be very tasteless and uninteresting without herbs, included either in the stuffing or in an accompanying sauce. A particularly good recipe is South African Soused Fish:

Soused Fish

1 onion
salt
boiling water
$1\frac{1}{2}$ lb (675g) any cold cooked fish

1 red pepper
6 allspice
3 bay leaves
6 coriander seeds
2 tablespoonsful olive oil
4 tablespoonsful vinegar

Slice the onion thinly, sprinkle with salt, pour a little boiling water over it, and leave it soaking. Arrange the fish in layers with the drained onion, spices, oil, and vinegar in a buttered pie-dish. Leave to stand for an hour. Cover the dish and stand it in a pan of hot water. Cook in a moderate oven for 20 minutes. The dish is excellent when served cold.

VEGETABLES
Herbs can be added to cooked vegetables, increasing and enhancing their flavour. Broad beans sprinkled with chopped basil or parsley, French beans with chopped parsley, tarragon, chervil, and chives, carrots with chopped mint, chives or parsley – the list is endless. Some herbs, like parsley and sorrel, can be used as a vegetable on their own. Parsley, which contains vitamin C, is a very useful addition to any savoury dish.

Fried Parsley
Wash the parsley and dry well in a cloth at least 1 hour before frying. The high water content of parsley causes hot fat to bubble fiercely and if the parsley is plunged straight into the fat and left there, the fat may boil over and cause a fire, so care must be taken when cooking. Put the parsley into the basket of a deep fat pan. Dip the basket just into the hot fat at 340°F (170°C), remove quickly, dip again and remove, then plunge into the fat and leave until most of the bubbling has ceased and the parsley is bright green and crisp. Drain on absorbent paper and serve.

Sorrel Purée

3 lb (1.5kg) sorrel
1 oz (25g) butter or margarine
salt and pepper
1-2 tablespoonsful cream
a little flour

Pick over the sorrel and wash it thoroughly. Place in a large saucepan with enough water to cover the bottom. Cook gently for about 20 minutes, turning it over and pressing it down repeatedly with a spoon to equalize the cooking. Drain and rub it through a fine sieve. Return it to the pan with the butter, cream and seasoning. Stir over heat for about 8 minutes, gradually adding enough flour to give a thick consistency. A little sugar can be added during cooking to counteract the acidity of the vegetable. Serve with egg or fish dishes.

MEAT DISHES
Casseroled Brisket or Silverside

1 lb (450g) brisket of beef (boned and rolled) or silverside
8 small carrots
3 small onions
3 young turnips
2 oz (50g) peas
$\frac{1}{4}$-$\frac{1}{2}$ pt (150-275ml) stock
bouquet of herbs (parsley, 3 or 4 mint leaves and 12 peppercorns)

Place the prepared vegetables, with herbs and peppercorns (tied in muslin), into a casserole dish with the meat and seasoning. Add hot stock to cover a quarter of the meat. Cook at Gas No.6/400°F (200°C) until simmering, lower temperature to Gas No.2/300°F (150°C) and continue to cook for about $1\frac{1}{2}$ hours. Add more stock if necessary as cooking proceeds. Serve with parsley dumplings.

Fricassée of Lamb

1 breast of lamb
1 onion
2 oz (50g) butter or margarine
2 bay leaves
a blade of mace
seasoning
1 pt (575ml) stock or water
1 oz (25g) flour
1 dessertspoonful capers
2 cloves
6 peppercorns

Cut the meat into 2-inch (5cm) squares. Melt the butter in a deep pan, and then add sliced onion, bay leaves, cloves, mace, peppercorns, seasoning, and meat. Cover and cook gently for about 30 minutes, stirring frequently. Add the boiling stock and simmer for 1 hour. Meanwhile, mix the flour with a little cold water to a smooth paste, add to it about $\frac{1}{2}$ pt (275ml) of the hot stock from the pan, return to the pan and simmer until the meat is tender. Serve on a hot dish and sprinkle the capers over the meat.

Grilled Spare Rib of Pork

6 chops from spare rib, tenderloin or neck
seasoning
sage
castor sugar
flour
stock
marjoram

Sprinkle both sides of the chops with a pinch of seasoning, sage, marjoram and castor sugar. Grill, turning frequently, until golden brown. Pour off the fat, add the flour and stock to make a thick gravy. Serve with apple sauce.

Liver Hot Pot

$\frac{1}{2}$ lb (225g) liver
seasoned flour
$\frac{1}{2}$ lb (225g) leeks
$\frac{1}{2}$ lb (225g) potatoes
3 small carrots
$\frac{1}{4}$ teaspoonful chopped sage
$\frac{1}{2}$ teaspoonful chopped parsley
seasoning
$\frac{3}{4}$ pt (425ml) stock
2-3 rashers of bacon

Grate the potatoes and carrots, shred leeks. Mix together three-quarters of the vegetables with the herbs and seasoning. Arrange in layers with the liver in a greased casserole, finishing with a layer of potato, and put the bacon on the top. Half fill with stock. Cover and bake for 45 minutes in a moderate oven.

Roast Chicken Stuffed with Herbs

1 chicken
1$\frac{1}{2}$ oz (37g) butter
Sauce
1 tablespoonful chopped onion
1 oz (25g) flour
seasoning
1 teaspoonful parsley
1 teaspoonful tarragon
2 tablespoonsful chopped carrot
$\frac{3}{4}$ pt (425ml) stock
1 glass white wine (optional)
1 teaspoonful chervil
Forcemeat
2 tablespoonsful breadcrumbs
1 teaspoonful chopped shallot
1 teaspoonful chopped tarragon

1 teaspoonful chopped parsley
1 teaspoonful chopped chervil
seasoning
liver from the chicken
1 oz (25g) melted butter

Mix the chopped liver with the breadcrumbs, herbs (forcemeat), seasoning, and sufficient melted butter to bind. Use this mixture to stuff the bird. Roast in a moderate oven for 1-$1\frac{1}{2}$ hours, depending on the weight.

To make the sauce, melt $1\frac{1}{2}$ oz (37g) butter, fry the onion and carrot, stir in the flour, and cook until lightly browned. Stir in the stock, bring to the boil, and add the seasoning, wine and herbs. Simmer for 15 minutes and serve.

DRINKS

Herbs can be used in many beverages and cups. Their flavour should not dominate the basic ingredients, but just add a little extra something. Leaves and flowers of herbs, such as the blue flowers of borage, provide an attractive garnish when floated on the surface. The following recipes are well worth a try, so 'here's to you!'

Apple Ginger

windfall apples
water
cloves
bay leaves
sugar
dry ginger ale
cucumber
mint leaves

Cut up the apples, add four cloves and half a bay leaf to every 2 lb

(900g) of apples, and stew in enough water to half cover the fruit until reduced to a pulp. Strain through muslin, and add sugar to taste. Chill. Add a $\frac{1}{3}$ pt (200ml) dry ginger ale to $\frac{2}{3}$ pt (400ml) apple juice. Serve with ice, sliced cucumber and mint leaves.

Lemon Mint Cordial

2 handfuls fresh mint
1$\frac{1}{2}$ pt (850ml) lemon squash
3 qt (3l) boiling water

Lightly crush the mint, and add to the lemon squash. Pour on the boiling water. Cool, then chill thoroughly before serving.

Bacchus Cup

$\frac{1}{2}$ bottle champagne
$\frac{1}{2}$ pt (275ml) sherry
$\frac{1}{8}$ pt (50ml) brandy
1 liqueur glassful noyeau
1 tablespoonful castor sugar
a few balm leaves
1 bottle soda water

Put everything except the soda water into a jug and let it stand for a few minutes. Add ice and soda water. Serve.

Claret Cup

1 bottle claret
thinly cut rind of a lemon
1-2 tablespoonsful castor sugar
1 wineglassful sherry
1 liqueur glassful brandy
1 liqueur glassful Maraschino
2-3 sprigs of balm, borage and verbena
1 large bottle soda water
1 liqueur glassful noyeau

Into a large jug put the claret, lemon rind and sugar. Cover and chill for 1 hour. Add the remaining ingredients, stir and serve.

For a relaxing drink to help you sleep, a herb tea is invaluable. Infuse leaves of balm, bergamot, chamomile, lemon verbena or southernwood in boiling water for a few minutes. Drink hot.

MEDICINAL RECIPES

Rue Tea (used for the relief of indigestion). Infuse a handful of rue leaves in 1 qt (1l) of boiling water. Leave to stand for 24 hours. Strain and bottle. Take a wineglassful each day.

Rosemary Tea (a refreshing tisane for colds in the head). Add a handful of rosemary, leaves and flowers, fresh or dried, to 1 pt (550ml) boiling water

Rosemary Scalp Tonic. Mix equal quantities of rosemary and southernwood with a quarter of the quantity by weight of camphor in 1pt (575ml) boiling water. Stand for 1 hour, strain and bottle. Rub a little into the scalp each day.

Hyssop Tea (a remedy for coughs, colds and sore throats). Make an infusion by using $\frac{1}{4}$ oz (6g) crushed dried leaves in 1 pt (575ml) boiling water. Leave for 15 minutes before using.

Chamomile Tea (used for insomnia and also as a tonic). To 1 pt (575ml) boiling water add a good handful of chamomile flowers, fresh or dried. Stand for 10 minutes before using.

Recipe for Pot-Pourri. Mix together 1 oz (25g) allspice, 1 oz (25g) cloves, 1oz (25g) ground nutmeg and 4 oz (100g) orris root. Add the juice and grated rind of 3 lemons. To this mixture add $1\frac{1}{2}$ oz (37g) oil of geranium, 1 oz (25g) essence of lemon, $\frac{1}{2}$ oz (12g) oil of bergamot and $\frac{1}{2}$ oz (12g) spirit of lavender. Gather handfuls of rose petals, dry them in the sun for an hour or two, mix with a few pinches of salt and salt-petre. Leave the two mixtures to stand for a few hours, then stir them together.

Put the mixture into a tightly-lidded container. Then, as more scented flowers and leaves become available, add them without drying first. Add more salt if the mixture becomes dry; it should remain moist. When, at the end of the season, no more flowers are available, stir the mixture again and decant into a bowl. The fragrance will last for quite a long time.

USEFUL ADDRESSES

Suppliers of Herbs

Ashfields Herb Nurseries, Hinstock, Market Drayton, Shropshire.

Augusta Seeds, Crown Chambers, 22 South St Mary's Gate, Grimsby, South Humberside.

Dorwest Herb Growers, Shipton Gorge, Bridport, Dorset.

The Herb Farm, Broad Oak Road, Canterbury, Kent.

Herbs From the Hoo, 46 Church Street, Buckden, Cambridgeshire.

Lighthorne Herbs, Lighthorne Rouch, Moreton Morrell, Warwick.

Oak Cottage Herb Farm, Nesscliffe, Shropshire.

Old Rectory Herb Farm, Ightham, Near Sevenoaks, Kent.

Stoke Lacy Herb Farm, Bromyard, Herefordshire.

Suffolk Herbs, Sawyers Farm, Little Cornard, Sudbury, Suffolk.

Tumblers Bottom Herb Farm, Kilmersdon, Radstock, Somerset.

Valeswood Herb Farm, Little Ness, Shropshire.

Yew Tree Herbs, Holt Street, Nonington, Nr Dover, Kent.

INDEX

RECIPE INDEX